IMAGES
of America

MANCHESTER-BY-THE-SEA

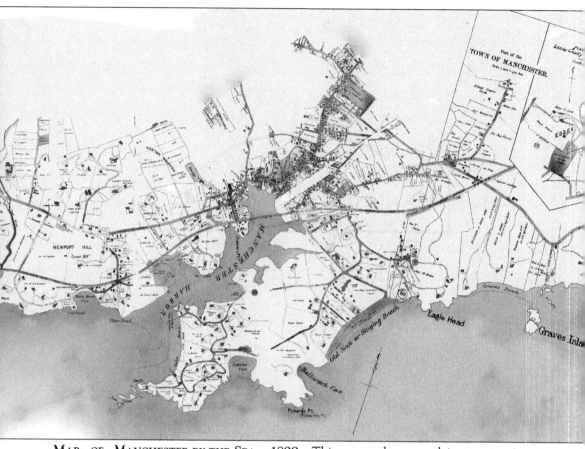

MAP OF MANCHESTER-BY-THE-SEA, 1899. This map shows outlying properties in Manchester-by-the-Sea that were originally farmland and are now occupied by numerous great estates from the Gilded Age. (Courtesy of the Manchester-by-the-Sea Public Library.)

On the cover: **PICNIC.** Families are seen picnicking on Singing Beach around 1915. Eagle Head, the rock outcrop in the background, is a well-known natural landmark. (Author's collection.)

IMAGES
of America

MANCHESTER-BY-THE-SEA

Stephen Roberts Holt

ARCADIA
PUBLISHING

Published by Arcadia Publishing
Charleston, South Carolina

Library of Congress Control Number: 2008929035

For all general information contact Arcadia Publishing at:
Telephone 843-853-2070
Fax 843-853-0044
E-mail sales@arcadiapublishing.com
For customer service and orders:
Toll-Free 1-888-313-2665

Visit us on the Internet at www.arcadiapublishing.com

To my children Anne and Stephen, whose Manchester ancestors arrived in the beginning; to those residents who are committed to maintaining the architectural integrity of this town; and to the firm of Roberts and Hoare, builders of the Gilded Age estates in Manchester-by-the-Sea

CONTENTS

Acknowledgments   6

Introduction   7

1.   Settlement of Cape Ann   9

2.   Jeffrey's Creek Becomes Manchester   17

3.   Manchester in the 1700s   23

4.   Manchester Builds   31

5.   The Summer Colony   51

6.   The Village   111

7.   The End of an Era   117

8.   Renewal   123

ACKNOWLEDGMENTS

Unless noted, all photographs in this book have come from the archives of the Manchester Historical Society. Its extensive collection of donated materials represents the community's generosity and commitment to preserving the legacy of this town.

Thank you to Esther "Slim" Proctor and her husband, Sherry Proctor. Esther, as the archivist for the historical society, was an invaluable consultant and advisor. This book could not have been written without her assistance. Sherry's too-numerous-to-be-listed contribution of time and creativity to the town of Manchester was and still is an inspiration to me.

Janice Holt, you were an enormous help to me in writing this book. Thank you for your many hours of work. Daryl Stoner, thank you for your research and dedication. Charles Rachal, thank you for your creativity, good humor, and long hours of work.

Gordon Abbott Jr., your informative book *Jeffrey's Creek* was an invaluable resource. Many thanks also go to Steve Rosenthal for photography, Kurt Wilhelm and Justin Demetri of the Essex Shipbuilding Museum, the Beverly Historical Society, and Elsie P. Youngman's book *Summer Echoes from the 19th Century, Manchester-by-the-Sea.*

INTRODUCTION

Manchester-by-the-Sea is a part of Cape Ann, located on Massachusetts's North Shore, and it is most famous for its Gilded Age summer resort. From 1845 to 1929, wealthy men who had amassed great fortunes during the expansion of the Industrial Revolution were looking to spend them on summer estates away from the city. Because there was no income tax, an elaborate house on an estate with a commanding view of rocky cove and the sea was an appealing and shrewd investment. Massive shingle-style and Colonial Revival cottages were built for families attracted to a soft primitivism where they could "rough it" as in the romanticized past but with a retinue of cooks, maids, and gardeners.

In their search for a truly American design form, architects during this age began to incorporate the simple shingled house design found along the New England coast, with new open-floor plans, creating larger, comfortable, and more sophisticated homes. These houses were ideally suited to their location, reaching out in many directions and following the contours of the rocky ledges. Large rooms with delicate detailing evoked the charm of an imagined early Colonial era, and generous porches and verandas that captured sea breezes created a wonderful atmosphere. In many ways, these grand houses re-created a past that never existed but were effective in providing a luxurious, peaceful retreat.

The rapid growth of the summer population marked the beginning of a dramatic expansion of Manchester's town environment and economy. As summer mansions were built, the village grew to support them. Electrical and water distribution systems, grocery stores, the first bank, livery stables, a lumberyard, a hardware store, a pharmacy, a rotunda, a horticultural hall, and yacht and country clubs all supported the services required by wealthy patrons.

The local building firm of Roberts and Hoare constructed all of these town buildings as an adjunct to the hundreds of estates and homes they were simultaneously constructing in the area. During its most active period, Roberts and Hoare employed over 200 men whose craftsmanship was due in part to the area's long tradition of shipbuilding and cabinetmaking. They built the summer estates represented in this book, including the famous Kragsyde and many others in Manchester and along the North Shore. The town flowered during this period, and much of what Roberts and Hoare accomplished remains intact in the Manchester-by-the-Sea that exists today.

Geographically, Manchester had everything people needed and wanted for leisure activities, including sandy beaches, a protected harbor and dramatic coastline, off-shore islands for yachting excursions, and train transportation that traveled to and from Boston. Singing Beach, with its rocky outcrop Eagle Head and white sand that verifiably sung a few notes on the musical scale, drew families seeking relief from the heat. It continues to be a popular destination for tourists and residents today.

Before there was a Manchester-by-the-Sea with its social and architectural prominence, there was a Native American camp and later a place named Jeffrey's Creek. The first attempt to establish a colony on Cape Ann was led by Roger Conant, who was a former member of the Plymouth Colony, in 1623. These original settlers established a fishing village north of Jeffrey's Creek. When hard economic conditions ended their venture in 1626, Conant led 30 desperate men to Salem. They passed by Jeffrey's Creek, which, in the future, became Manchester-by-the-Sea.

During this time, the Massachusetts Bay charter was granted by King Charles I of England to Sir Richard Saltonstall and newly appointed governor John Winthrop. Both influential merchants, they sailed to the New World on the ship *Arbella*, looking for new opportunities. In 1630, the *Arbella* anchored in Massachusetts Bay near Jeffrey's Creek where several homes had been built on land granted from Salem. In 1645, the Massachusetts Bay Colony gave the village its independence and, along with it, the name Manchester. By 1700, fishermen and lumber traders were sailing their cargos throughout the bay area, and the town was growing in size.

Fishing and coastal trade was Manchester's principal source of income until the beginning of the Revolutionary War. The harbor, little more than an estuary, was ideally suited to small-boat fishermen who could easily haul their vessels up on the grassy coastal banks. As Manchester sea captains prospered and their ships increased in size, they were moored in the deepwater harbors of Beverly and Gloucester. With prosperity, the town's architecture became more sophisticated. Georgian details began to appear on existing houses, and by the end of the Revolutionary War, new homes were built in the delicate Federal style.

After the Revolutionary War and the War of 1812, Manchester's fishing fleet was in a shambles. Small boats were quickly built, but without a deepwater harbor, fishing and shipping could no longer support the town's economy, and families turned to cabinetmaking. This industry prospered into the 1960s, producing furniture that reflected each period of the decorative arts. Manchester, although rural, was becoming wealthy, and the classical Greek Revival houses in town were symbolic of a new sophistication.

When train tracks were laid from Beverly to Manchester in 1845, the town began to attract summer visitors. By the mid-1800s, modest summer cottages were being built on the coast for the wealthy residents of Salem and Boston. Manchester's Gilded Age had started. From 1850 to 1929, the area was transformed into a socially prominent summer resort. By the late 1800s, the old saltwater farms had disappeared, and the great estates with massive shingle-style houses took their place. Manchester was a destination for lavish living. Yachts, country clubs, beaches, and massive hotels provided well-heeled summer residents arriving from Washington, D.C., Chicago, and Pittsburgh a rich lifestyle until the beginning of the Great Depression and World War II.

After World War II, Manchester was slow to recover, as society was more mobile and pragmatic, and there seemed to be no need for a summer-long vacation in Manchester-by-the-Sea. The magnificent summer cottages were deemed outmoded and unfashionable. In fact, any building that was not modern seemed to be fair game for the wrecker's ball. The practice of lopping off the top floors of buildings with all their dormers and towers was common in this area during the 1950s and 1960s, and the integrity of the town was at stake.

Presently the opportunity for new ideas abounds in Manchester. Since the early settlers landed at Jeffrey's Creek, ingenuity has been a source of community pride. The town developed, fortunes were made and lost, the Gilded Age came and went, and Manchester-by-the-Sea remains. With the integrity and commitment inherited from these earlier generations, Manchester might pause to consider its legacy as residents continue to invent their future.

One

SETTLEMENT OF
CAPE ANN

ROGER CONANT. Cape Ann's first
colony was established in 1623 by Roger
Conant (1592–1679). He was a former
member of the Plymouth Colony that was
settled by the Pilgrims three years earlier
in 1620. The bronze statue is by artist
Henry H. Kitson and is located in Salem.

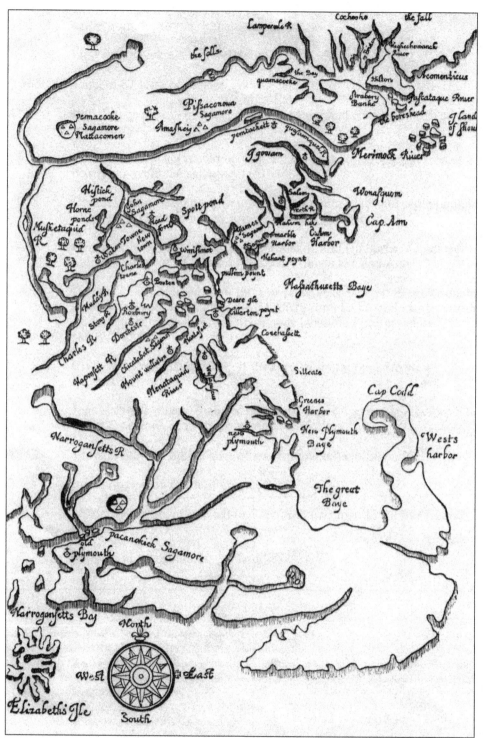

EARLY NEW ENGLAND MAP, 1634. A guide for would-be settlers, William Wood's map is from his book *New England Prospects*. Dated 1634, it is the oldest-known map showing details of Boston and Cape Ann on Massachusetts Bay. (Courtesy of the City of Gloucester.)

MASSACHUSETTS BAY, C. 1830. An idealized view of Massachusetts Bay in 1630 was painted on the side of a Boston fire engine. (Courtesy of the Bostonian Society.)

PAINTING OF CHIEF MASCONOMO, 1895. A fabricated portrait of Chief Masconomo was painted by William H. Tappan in 1895 to commemorate the 250th anniversary of the town. Masconomo was a sagamore of Agawam and a local Native American chief who welcomed the first British settlers to Cape Ann in 1630.

SIR RICHARD SALTONSTALL.
Sir Richard Saltonstall (1586–1658) was one of the original grantees of the Massachusetts Bay Company. He left England in 1630 aboard the *Arbella* and upon arriving was the first assistant to Gov. John Winthrop. Although he remained in Massachusetts for only a short time, his descendants played a major role in New England history. (Courtesy of the Massachusetts Historical Society.)

MASSACHUSETTS BAY CHARTER, 1629. The charter was granted by King Charles I of England to the backers of an influential group of merchants. Among them was Sir Richard Saltonstall. They acquired the patent authority of the king in March 1629 and created the governor and company of the Massachusetts Bay in New England. (Courtesy of the Massachusetts Historical Society.)

JOHN WINTHROP. An artist from the school of Sir Anthony Van Dyck painted this portrait between 1625 and 1649 of John Winthrop (1588–1649). Winthrop arrived on the *Arbella* with Saltonstall and was elected the first governor of the Massachusetts Bay Colony in 1630. According to Howard Zinn's *A People's History of the United States*, the Massachusetts Bay Colony's land was taken from Native Americans with Winthrop's excuse that they had not "subdued" the land and thus had no "civil right" to it. (Courtesy of the American Antiquarian Society.)

THE ARBELLA. In April 1630, Winthrop sailed from England on the *Arbella*, which was accompanied by six other ships and 300 settlers bound for Massachusetts Bay. On Tuesday, June 10, 1630, the *Arbella* dropped anchor near Jeffrey's Creek, which at the time was a part of Salem. The landing of the *Arbella* marked the beginning of what historians call the great migration. (Courtesy of the Peabody Essex Museum.)

13

EAGLE HEAD, 1890. This rough weather on Eagle Head shows conditions similar to the ones faced by the early settlers. Continuous storms battered the coast and made fishing difficult. In order to survive, men had to go to sea in these conditions, with many never returning. Severe weather shaped the character of these early fishermen, forging what has come to be known as the New England temperament.

SHALLOP. An improvement over the first canoes purchased from the Native Americans, this small 25- to 45-foot-long versatile, heavily constructed workboat was used to explore and map the coastline and conduct trade with the tribes of the region. Shallops played an essential role in the survival of the settlements in the New World. This image is from the 1839 ledger of Samuel G. Randall. (Courtesy of Douglas B. Sharp.)

PIONEER VILLAGE, SALEM. This re-created village in Salem was built in 1930 for the tercentenary celebration of the 1630 arrival of John Winthrop on the *Arbella*. This photograph shows what the earliest shelters were like in Salem and in Jeffrey's Creek. These dugouts and English wigwams were necessary for the men to survive the harsh weather while they were building their wood-frame houses. (Author's collection.)

PIONEER VILLAGE, 1930. This photograph shows another view of the re-created village. The *Arbella* is docked near several simple wood-framed structures. The roofs of the houses are thatched in salt hay from the marsh, as the settlers of Jeffrey's Creek would have done when they first arrived. Within a short period of time, these houses rapidly became more sophisticated in order to better endure the New England weather. (Author's collection.)

A 250TH ANNIVERSARY, 1895. These costumed men are pictured on the Manchester Yacht Club dock before embarking on a replica of the *Arbella*. They are representing Gov. John Winthrop (second from the right) and the Puritans who arrived with him in 1630. They are celebrating the founding of Jeffrey's Creek, whose name was changed to Manchester in 1645.

REENACTMENT OF THE 1630 LANDING OF WINTHROP, 1895. A replica of the *Arbella* (not shown) was towed to the inner harbor where the men disembarked and rowed to a platform over the tidal marsh. Greeting them was Chief Masconomo (played by police sergeant Leonard Andrews) and the people, celebrating the 250th anniversary of the town. (Author's collection.)

Two

JEFFREY'S CREEK
BECOMES MANCHESTER

**YE 400 ACRES
MAP.** By 1636,
a few families
built homes at
Jeffrey's Creek on
land granted to
them from Salem.
Most of them
were freemen and
entitled to property
in these common
lands, known as
the 400 acres. They
acquired parcels
ranging from 30
to 60 acres. The
area on this map
was called Jeffrey's
Creek, named after
the Jeffrey's Ledge
fishing grounds.
(Courtesy of
D. F. Lamson.)

ENGRAVING OF FORSTER'S WHARF, C. 1895. The beginnings of Manchester harbor are illustrated in this engraving by Kilburn and Cross after a watercolor by W. H. Tappan. Forster's Wharf sits "by the thread of Bennett's Brook." Here the coastline swept inward, forming a shallow, protected harbor practical for the small-boat fisherman. This estuary was well suited for drying fish and building and launching boats. In the future, the boats in this engraving, the Chebacco, pinkie, and Grand Banker, formed the backbone of coastal trade and fishing in Manchester. (Courtesy of D. F. Lamson.)

FORSTER'S MILL. By 1700, the town built a schoolhouse, a sawmill, a blacksmith shop, and the Forster's tide mill sitting at the mouth of Bennett's Brook. The coastline of coves and islands covered in pine, cedar, and oak provided construction materials, and the abundant Cape Ann granite became the foundation for buildings.

MODEL OF A CHEBACCO BOAT, THE SALEM. The construction of the shallop evolved, with time, into Chebacco boats, which were a bigger and heavier craft for fishing and trade. By the end of the 18th century, Chebacco boats were famous up and down the New England coast. (Courtesy of the Essex Shipbuilding Museum, Dana Story Collection.)

FISH FLAKES. Codfish was salted and then dried in the sun on wooden racks, called fish flakes. At the time, it was the only way of preserving a large catch of fish for later consumption or for trading. (Courtesy of the National Park Service, Maritime Salem in the Age of Sail.)

PEARSE-MAY HOUSE, BUILT AROUND 1670. A typical saltbox house, the Pearse-May house shows evidence of additional growth, which was common in the early 17th century for expanding families that in many cases had 15 people living under one roof. The addition had a two-story front face with windows facing south. The steeper pitched roof to the north gave protection from the winter winds. The current residents believe that a friendly ghost from the 17th-century Pearse family still inhabits the house. (Author's collection.)

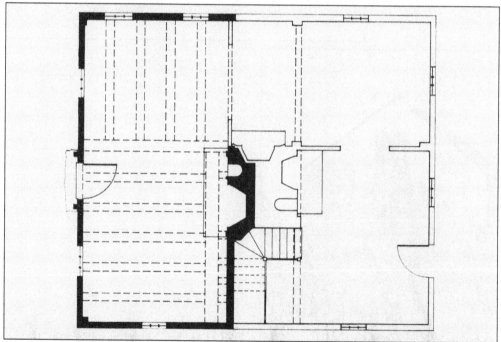

PLAN OF PEARSE-MAY HOUSE, BUILT AROUND 1670. In this floor plan, the first bay was taken from the frame of an older house built in 1640. A second bay is placed in line with the first, extending the house another 10 feet. At a later date, the kitchen was moved from the hall to the back of the chimney. The chimney itself was enlarged to provide a new cooking area, and the hall, with its large chimney for heating, became an additional room. A more fully developed staircase led to additional sleeping space on the second floor. (Author's collection.)

ABBY-BAKER HOUSE, BUILT IN 1690. This rugged saltbox was located near what eventually became the center of town. It stood for over two centuries, partly due to its heavy timber-frame construction. Most of these early homes were built of oak. Extreme difficulty was involved in shaping and handling it, but once put in place, it undeniably stayed put. The Bakers were an old Manchester family who farmed land that is now part of the Essex County Club golf course. (Author's collection.)

THE BENNETT-ROBERTS HOUSE, BUILT IN 1675. Another example of saltbox construction, the Bennett-Roberts house is situated on a slope above Bennett's Brook. The hill was used by generations for a sledding hill until the application of salt and sand on winter roads ruined the tradition.

THE STANLEY-ALLEN HOUSE, BUILT IN 1780. Built on Forest Street, the simplicity of the Stanley-Allen house's landscape is typical of those in the late 1600s. Both the Stanley and Allen families eventually cleared the land for modest farming and cordwood. They removed the fieldstones for stone walls and house foundations. These early settlers used approximately 13 cords of wood to survive the winter, leaving the town landscape open, with firewood being brought in from woodlots outside town.

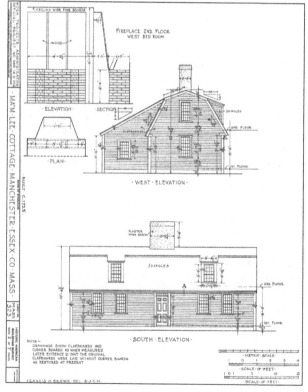

THE LEE COTTAGE, BUILT IN THE LATE 1600s. This house belonged to the Lee family for more than a century. Isaac Lee, the first owner of the house, was captain of a privateer during the Revolutionary War. The last family member to occupy the house, aunt Sarah Lee, was a character who smoked a pipe, planted and sold herbs, and was so successful that some people called her a witch doctor. These hand-drawn elevations were done by the Historic American Building Survey, a Works Progress Administration Depression-era project. (Courtesy of the Library of Congress.)

Three

MANCHESTER
IN THE 1700s

WATERCOLOR OF A PINKIE, C. 1900.
By 1700, Manchester fishermen were moving beyond the boundaries of Massachusetts Bay and venturing farther out toward George's Bank. Coastal trade expanded as well, and a large number of vessels engaged in carrying lumber and goods along the coast. By the end of the 18th century, schooners sailed Canadian waters, fishing for cod and trading in the West Indies and Europe. With prosperity, the craftsmen were flourishing and homes were being built with greater sophistication. (Courtesy of the Essex Shipbuilding Museum, Dana Story Collection.)

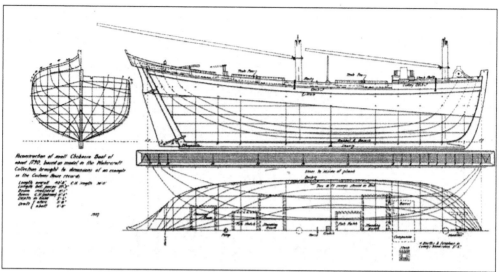

CONSTRUCTION PLANS FOR A PINKIE, DRAWN IN 1804. The natural evolution of the Chebacco boat created the famous type known as the pinkie. These plans show that it was a distinctive type of schooner with bulwarks swept upward to a high triangular pinked stern. The average 50-foot pinkie carried a crew of six, including the skipper. (Courtesy of the Essex Shipbuilding Museum, Dana Story Collection.)

MODEL OF A PINKIE, 1820. It is thought that the pinkie was among the most seaworthy vessels ever designed, a tribute to its Essex and Manchester shipbuilders. Its hull was narrow in the stern, it was buoyant as a barrel forward, and it rode the seas like a duck. It was the safest and most sought-after boat all along the East Coast. (Courtesy of Mystic Seaport.)

THE BUILDING OF A GRAND BANKS SCHOONER. As Manchester sea captains began to require larger fishing vessels, they turned to the famous Story Shipyard in Essex. Here in this 1880 photograph is an unidentified vessel being framed in typical Essex boat construction with double-sawn oak frames fastened by wooden pegs. As they were too big for Manchester's shallow harbor, they were moored in Gloucester. (Courtesy of the Essex Shipbuilding Museum, Dana Story Collection.)

WATERCOLOR OF THE SARAH FRANKLIN, 1846. The *Sarah Franklin* was typical of schooners of the day and would have been called a banker. Schooners were designed for speed and a quick return trip from the Grand Banks, as ice, rather than salt, was now used to preserve the fish. The patches on the *Sarah Franklin's* sails reflect an economy-minded skipper. (Courtesy of the Essex Shipbuilding Museum, Dana Story Collection.)

DEACON BINGHAM HOUSE, BUILT IN 1754. This house is typical of provincial Georgian architecture. There is a formal arrangement of windows and doors in their symmetrical composition, which is enriched by the classically detailed doorway. Dea. D. L. Bingham filled many town offices. He was town clerk for 29 years, a representative of the general court, a deacon of the church for 32 years, and the first postmaster of the town, holding the office for 34 years.

THE LOW HOUSE, BUILT IN 1690. The Low house, a small house originally built by John Knight, gradually was rebuilt to become a larger and more refined example of Georgian architecture. It has a cornice placed over the window casings, a triangular pediment, an entablature, and pilasters surrounding the centrally placed front door. It was later occupied by Dea. A. E. Low and was taken down in 1890.

KITFIELD HOUSE DOORWAY, BUILT IN 1768. The doorway in this house reflects the influence of English pattern books on early Georgian American architecture. Where these book details are traditionally illustrated as stone, the colonists executed them in the abundantly available wood. This doorway, built by a Kitfield, was a typical and inexpensive way to embellish the architecture of a provincial house. (Author's collection.)

GEORGIAN DETAILS, 1728. The Georgian doorway and cornice details, from James Gibbs's pattern book *A Book of Architecture* (1728), are typical of what was copied from this and numerous other English pattern books to accommodate demand in the colonies by the newly affluent desiring more fashionable homes. (Author's collection.)

KITFIELD HOUSE FACADE, BUILT IN 1768. The Kitfield home housed a family famous for seafaring adventures. During the Revolutionary War, William Kitfield, age 21, and two other men on a return voyage from Spain were taken by a British ship of war and imprisoned in England. They escaped and shipped out on a vessel bound for Halifax, Nova Scotia. While onshore, each one bought a sword and later took over the ship. They were eventually rescued by an American privateer and returned to Salem. (Author's collection.)

HOOPER HOUSE FACADE, BUILT AROUND 1770. This house has a refined doorway, which was more than likely influenced by James Gibbs's pattern book *A Book of Architecture* (1728). It was owned by Manchester's first physician-surgeon, Dr. Joseph Whipple. (Author's collection.)

PEARSE-MAY HOUSE. By 1750, the Pearse-May house that had been a saltbox (see page 20) grew in size and architectural stature by adding a full second floor and a new Georgian doorway. Early New Englanders were frugal and would add on rather than tear down. When John Pearse built the house, it was sited next to a three-story granite outcrop known as Norton's Mountain, protecting it from violent Northeast storms. (Author's collection.)

BROWN-GIRDLER HOUSE, BUILT IN 1775. This house, built at the start of the Revolutionary War on a high point of land on the old road to Gloucester, has a particularly fine Georgian entryway. Travelers that stopped at John Allen's tavern across the street rested their horses in a barn behind this house. (Author's collection.)

MARSTERS-TUCK HOUSE, BUILT BETWEEN 1725 AND 1733. This well-proportioned Georgian home had four rooms on each floor and a chimney on either side of the center hall. There were eight fireplaces. The first owner, Nathanial Marsters, was a fisherman with a warehouse and wharf on what is now known as Tucks Point. The house was then sold in 1785 to William Tuck, a privateer in the Revolutionary War and the commander of the *Remington*. When Tuck retired, he became a farmer and large landholder in the town. (Author's collection.)

Four

MANCHESTER BUILDS

WATERCOLOR OF THE PRIVATEER FAME, 1804. The Revolutionary period covering the second' half of the 18th century was a period of general upheaval. Many of Manchester's men went to sea on privateers. Fast-sailing American privateers with letters of marque, which legalized their actions as independently owned vessels, attacked and captured British merchantmen who were carrying valuable supplies to their troops. They played a vital role in winning the country's independence. The *Fame* was one of the more famous privateers. (Courtesy of the Essex Shipbuilding Museum, Dana Story Collection.)

POWDER HOUSE, BUILT IN 1810. Continued conflict with Britain and interference with maritime trade precipitated the War of 1812. The first warlike measure adopted in Manchester was to build a fort on Norton's Point with a view to the entrance of the harbor. In addition, a powder house was built on a town hill overlooking the village, known as Powder House Hill. There was no active conflict in Manchester; however, the privateers were continually looking for British ships.

PRIVATEER, c. 1800. This ship is typical of the fast-moving American privateers that preyed upon English shipping. Due to Manchester's shallow waters, there were no vessels of this size that sailed from the harbor, but Manchester men were on privateers from Salem and Beverly. Six thousand British prisoners were taken in the War of 1812. America was becoming a strong presence on the sea. (Courtesy of the Peabody Essex Museum.)

FORSTER-LEACH HOUSE, BUILT IN 1804. Maj. Israel Forster built this house in the Federal style. The enclosed entry porch exemplifies the Federal architectural style that was popular at the end of the Revolutionary War. New Englanders of this period were drawn to the delicacy and grace of the neoclassic Adams style, made popular by the Asher Benjamin pattern books. (Courtesy of the Historic American Building Survey.)

FORSTER-LEACH HOUSE FACADE, BUILT IN 1804. The monitor roof with a widow's walk and fine classical proportions makes this house an elegant example of Federal architecture. This house was occupied by the Forster and Leach families until the late 1900s. Capt. Thomas Leach, born in 1807, went to sea as a cabin boy at the age of nine. For 51 years, he traveled on voyages all over the world, including to Russia and China. He escaped pirates in East India and lived to tell these exciting tales of his seafaring adventures. (Courtesy of the Historic American Building Survey.)

THE FIRST PARISH CHURCH, CONGREGATIONAL, BUILT IN 1809. This elegant architectural steeple design is attributed to Col. Jacob John Smith. Pattern books were used by local carpenters in the early 1800s to give buildings sophistication and style. (Courtesy of Dick Towle.)

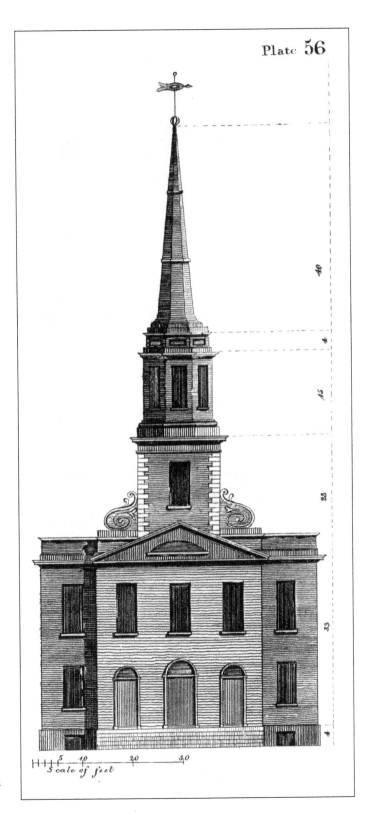

ELEVATION, THE
AMERICAN BUILDERS
COMPANION, 1806. A
notable example of Asher
Benjamin's influence
is the sophisticated
Congregational church
where the framing is
typically Colonial and
similar to a New England
barn, but the exterior
sheathing is of thinner
clapboards. The delicately
refined details with
sophisticated pilasters
and doorway are typical
of the late Federal period.
(Courtesy of the American
Builders Companion.)

Plate 56

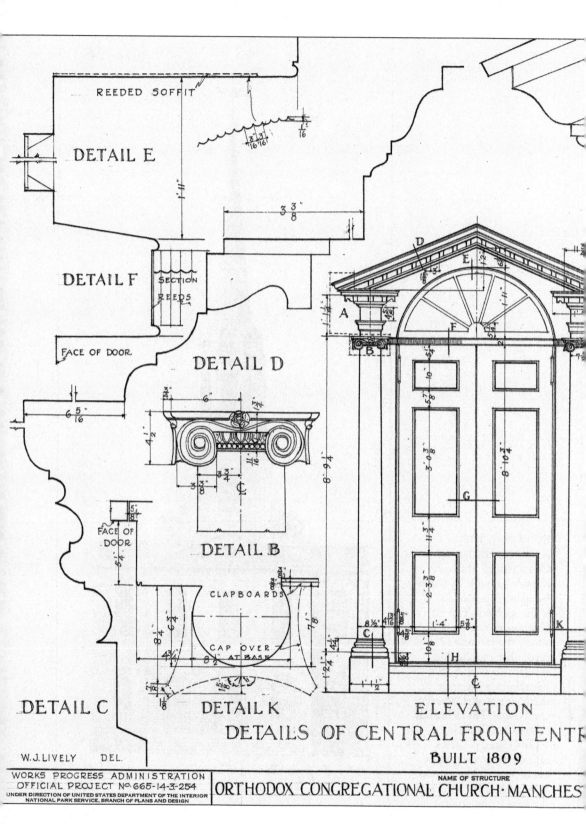

REEDED SOFFIT

DETAIL E

DETAIL F

SECTION

REEDS

FACE OF DOOR

DETAIL D

DETAIL B

FACE OF
DOOR

CLAPBOARDS

CAP OVER
AT BASE

DETAIL C

DETAIL K

ELEVATION

DETAILS OF CENTRAL FRONT ENTR

BUILT 1809

W. J. LIVELY   DEL.

WORKS PROGRESS ADMINISTRATION
OFFICIAL PROJECT Nº 665-14-3-254
UNDER DIRECTION OF UNITED STATES DEPARTMENT OF THE INTERIOR
NATIONAL PARK SERVICE, BRANCH OF PLANS AND DESIGN

NAME OF STRUCTURE
ORTHODOX CONGREGATIONAL CHURCH·MANCHES

36

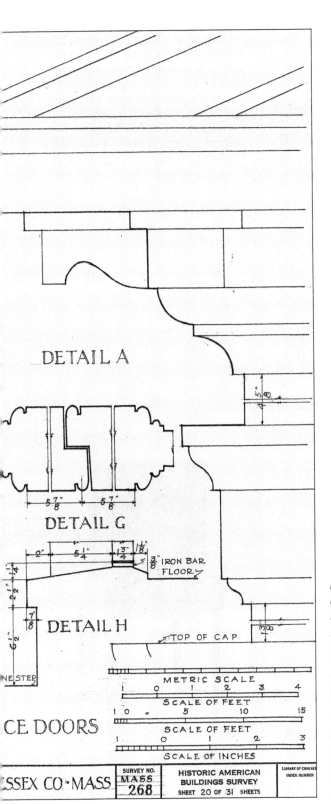

DETAIL A

DETAIL G

5⅞" 5⅞"

2" 5¼" 1¾" ⅛" IRON BAR
⅜ FLOOR

DETAIL H

⅞

TOP OF CAP

NE STEP

CE DOORS

METRIC SCALE
0 1 2 3 4

SCALE OF FEET
1 0 5 10 15

SCALE OF FEET
1 0 1 2 3

SCALE OF INCHES

SSEX CO·MASS

	SURVEY NO.	HISTORIC AMERICAN	LIBRARY OF CONGRESS INDEX NUMBER
	MASS 268	BUILDINGS SURVEY SHEET 20 OF 31 SHEETS	

ORTHODOX CONGREGATIONAL CHURCH, 1809. These front door details were drawn by the Historic American Building Survey in 1934. Since the 1930s, the Historic American Building Survey has produced measured drawings, photographs, and written data for a national architectural archive. These details are a vivid example of the craftsman's skills and a testament to the sophistication of the emerging cabinetmaking industry of Manchester. (Courtesy of the Historic American Building Survey.)

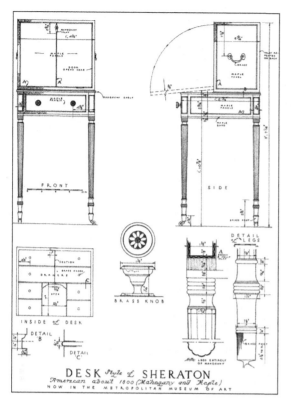

DESK *Style of* SHERATON
American about 1800 (Mahogany and Maple)
NOW IN THE METROPOLITAN MUSEUM OF ART

DRAWING OF A LADY'S WRITING DESK, C. 1800. The detailing on the lady's writing desk shows the refinement of Manchester's famous cabinetmaking. Notice a similar sophistication in this small-scale drawing to the previous Congregational church doorway drawing. (Courtesy of the Metropolitan Museum of Art.)

SHERATON WRITING DESK, BUILT AROUND 1800. This unusual piece of furniture is a lady's writing desk in the Sheraton style. Its slender construction reflects the Federal architecture of the time. (Courtesy of the Metropolitan Museum of Art.)

HAND-CARVED DETAIL. This hand-carved detail on a *c.* 1835 mahogany side chair at the Manchester Historical Society shows the capabilities of Manchester craftsmen. Manchester was also well known for producing veneers. John Perry Allen was one of the first in the United States to perfect a machine that could cut a four-inch-thick plank into 100 veneers.

MANCHESTER CRAFTSMAN, C. 1880. Most of Manchester's fishing fleet was destroyed during the Revolutionary War, and the remaining sea captains kept their large mercantile ships in the deeper harbors of Gloucester, Salem, and Beverly. Although Manchester continued coastal fishing on a small scale, it now focused on the more profitable cabinetmaking. During its most active period, there were 43 different furniture mills employing hundreds of workers. In this photograph, a craftsman works with a reeding and fluting machine to create a Sheraton table leg.

CHARLES LEE CABINET MILL, C. 1864. Furniture was sent as far south as New Orleans from Charles Lee's three-story cabinet mill. The furniture-making industry in Manchester started with Moses Dodge in 1760 and lasted until the 1960s, producing furniture that reflected the decorative arts of each architectural period.

CAPT. RICHARD TRASK AND ABIGAIL HOOPER TRASK, C. 1840. During their lifetimes, Capt. Richard Trask and Abigail Hooper Trask were very accomplished people. Abigail owned a store selling fashionable women's finery. She built her own house, which is now the home of the historical society, and her opinion was so valued that the town selectmen consulted her on a regular basis. At the age of 35, she married Richard and had a child one year later. The captain was a prosperous and well-respected man.

THE ST. PETERSBURG, 1839. Capt. Richard Trask was one of 50 masters of merchant vessels living in town by 1816. This painting at the Manchester Historical Society is his ship, the *St. Petersburg*. It was co-owned by Enoch Train and Company of Boston and was moored in Boston Harbor. The *St. Petersburg* was built in 1839 and, at the time, was the largest vessel ever built in Massachusetts.

ABIGAIL HOOPER TRASK HOUSE, BUILT IN 1823. Abigail Hooper built this house prior to her marriage to Capt. Richard Trask. Abigail, a successful businesswoman, also acted as an attorney. This building is now home to the Manchester Historical Society. This house embodies the Greek Revival style of architecture that grew out of an admiration for the ancient culture of classical Greece.

THE MARBLE-KITFIELD HOUSE. The dawn of the 19th century saw the advent of Greek Revival architecture, a period from 1800 to 1860, during which the town rapidly expanded. The typical structure had a bold silhouette with a classic temple front and pilasters or columns. This house was built in 1836 for one of Manchester's prosperous cabinetmakers, George Marble. It was later purchased in 1871 by the seafaring Kitfields, who owned an adjacent property. (Author's collection.)

Greek Revival Buildings. Examples of three different versions of the popular Greek Revival style were built in a row. The Kitfield house sits on the far right with large free-standing columns. The middle house shows a more modified version with pilasters instead of columns. An earlier Colonial home on the left shows the now-popular addition of a frieze board (above the second-floor windows) and two modest Greek Revival doorways.

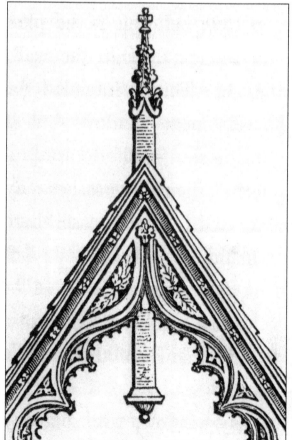

Gable End, Gothic Revival Verge Board. By 1850, the rules of ancient Greece were set aside for the romantic appeal of England's medieval past. Manchester has few remaining Gothic Revival buildings, perhaps because the town was removed from the mainstream of urban life and favored the simpler and easier-to-build Greek Revival house. (Courtesy of *The Architecture of Country Houses*, by Andrew Jackson Downing.)

HENRY KITFIELD HOUSE, BUILT IN 1847. Built in the very fashionable Gothic Revival style by Henry Kitfield, this house sat on an expanse of waterfront land where he had his own wharf. It was painted a stony-gray color in an attempt to make the wood appear to be masonry. Characteristic Gothic elements are the heavy door with cast-iron hinges and steeply pitched cross-gable roofs. The references to medieval English domestic architecture are numerous. Kitfield was 31 years old and a prominent and wealthy businessman at the time he married Lucy Ann Danforth, who is pictured here seated with her daughter and grandchildren.

EMMANUEL CHURCH CHAPEL, BUILT IN 1882. A Gothic Revival chapel was built in 1882 with funding from Civil War major Russell Sturgis Jr. Early in the Civil War, he raised a company of men for the Union army in Manchester. The church was a gift to his wife.

EASTERN RAILROAD TERMINAL. The Eastern Railroad terminal in Boston, complete with a tower, is at the far right. In the foreground is the Boston and Lowell Railroad station. The Eastern Railroad line brought train service to Manchester and Cape Ann in 1845. Transportation and communication made changes nationwide as well as in Manchester-by-the-Sea. (Courtesy of the Beverly Historical Society, Walker Collection.)

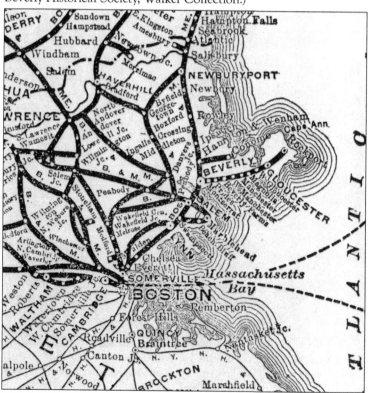

EASTERN RAILROAD LINE. A map of the Eastern Railroad line shows the original route from Boston to Portsmouth, New Hampshire. It was built in the 1830s, and the line from Beverly to Manchester and Cape Ann was established in 1845. (Courtesy of the Beverly Historical Society, Walker Collection.)

LOCOMOTIVE NO. 24. The *Beverly*, locomotive No. 24, is leaving the castlelike Salem station headed for Manchester. This fanciful station was a celebration of this new mode of transportation. (Courtesy of the Beverly Historical Society, Walker Collection.)

Depot, Manchester-by-the-Sea, Mass.

MANCHESTER RAILROAD STATION. The station was built in the Richardsonian style, with extensive covered waiting platforms necessary for visitors arriving in private parlor cars. Albert C. Burrage arrived each year from California in his Pullman car, which had seven staterooms, private baths, a living room, a dining room, a galley, and quarters for the staff. As Manchester-by-the-Sea was a summer destination for the wealthy and famous, great pride was taken in maintaining the beautifully landscaped and manicured grounds. (Courtesy of the Beverly Historical Society, Walker Collection.)

CIVIL WAR VETERANS, 1898. A total of 159 Manchester men served in the Civil War in 10 different infantry regiments as well as in the cavalry and naval units. Here is a gathering in 1898 of Manchester's veterans of the war.

SONS OF UNION VETERANS, 1900. The men assembled in front of the Manchester Memorial Library are from the Sons of Union Veterans, Allen Post 67, Grand Army of the Republic.

MANCHESTER PUBLIC LIBRARY, 1887. The public library was the gift of summer resident Thomas Jefferson Coolidge in memory of Manchester's Union forces that served during the Civil War. At the dedication, it was named the Memorial Library and Grand Army Hall. Designed by noted architect Charles McKim, the library is an example of his early romantic style and inspired by his extensive studies in France.

THOMAS JEFFERSON COOLIDGE, 1877. A direct descendant of the nation's third president, Thomas Jefferson Coolidge was a generous benefactor to the town of Manchester. He was a well-traveled financier, philanthropist, and future ambassador to France. He generously gave of his time and money to build the town library, the town water system, and land for the Essex County Club.

TOWN VIEW FROM POWDER HOUSE HILL, 1850. By now, downtown Manchester was well delineated. It looks generally as it does today, with its road patterns, the village green and the Congregational church, the Trask house, Knight's wharf, and small stores. The inner harbor was still undredged, accessible only at high tide. Manchester men continued to fish the local waters, but the economy was centered on the cabinetmaking industry.

VIEW OF DANA'S BEACH, LATE 1800S. In the foreground is Richard Henry Dana Sr.'s house. He acquired this land in 1845 and became Manchester's first summer resident. The shingled house on the point of land in the distance was built by Richard Henry Dana Jr., who wrote *Two Years Before the Mast*. This house was moved in 1901 to become the gardener's cottage of the larger Felsenmere.

Five

THE SUMMER COLONY

LOW TIDE, BY WINSLOW HOMER, 1873. Manchester's Singing Beach was immortalized in this famous painting. Many artists, including Winslow Homer, Charles Hopkinson, John F. Kensett, Fitz Henry (Hugh) Lane, and Edward Hopper, painted extensively in the Cape Ann area, capturing the rugged, granite coastline and the working lives of fishermen. By the late 19th century, when the wealthy came to play in Manchester, a defined social network began to develop. Their society became known as Manchester's summer colony. (Courtesy of the Metropolitan Museum of Art.)

SUMMER COTTAGE, 1876. The first summer residents, known as rusticators, arrived in Manchester from communities as close as Salem, which at the time was an urban center in Massachusetts. This cottage, designed for J. W. Merritt, is typical of Manchester's first seasonal summer residences built in the stick style. Portions of the frame were left exposed on the exterior as a decorative feature, thus the name stick style, which was made popular by Andrew Jackson Downing in his influential book *The Architecture of Country Houses.*

MAGNOLIA RAILROAD STATION, 1896. The influence of the stick style is seen even on this Manchester-by-the-Sea railroad station near Gloucester. The station was especially busy in the summer months when visitors flocked to the nearby fashionable summer colony of Magnolia, where they stayed in large shingled hotels by the sea. It was destroyed in 1942.

CHUBBS, 1873. This house is named after Thomas Chubbs, an early settler who lived on Chubbs Point in 1636. Chubbs was one of the first stick-style houses in Manchester. Externally, it was an unpretentious structure with a small square tower on its appealing, homey front and offered the seasonal visitor a modest house for a simple life by the sea. This new style, with its honesty in structural detail, heralded the beginnings of a truly American style of architecture. Only a few were built in Manchester, and this last remaining example was destroyed in 2008.

INTERIOR OF CHUBBS, 1873. A fine example of a stick-style interior is seen here. These rooms tended to be picturesque but simple. Heavily embellished by shelving and china, the interior, including organic wallpapers, shows the influence of William Morris.

PAINTING OF INNER HARBOR, 1880. The painting of the inner harbor by an unknown artist shows Knight's lumber and coal wharf, and a distant view of the Smith farm on Smith's Point. The surrounding landscape looks like the Maine coast with rocks, scrubby trees, and indigenous plant material. Manchester was essentially a small farming and fishing community with extensive open land prior to the town's expansion.

SMITH FARM, SMITH'S POINT, LATE 1800s. The Smith family lived in a Greek Revival house on a saltwater farm. Here the lack of trees and open farmland is noticeable. In fact, all of Smith's Point and land adjacent to the town was originally used for cultivation.

REV. CYRUS AUGUSTUS BARTOL, C. 1865. Rev. Cyrus Augustus Bartol, a minister of Boston's Old West Church, was a summer visitor who saw the potential for Manchester's growth as a summer colony. He rented here before purchasing Smith's Point, Norton's Point, and Tucks Point, which he later sold or developed for a substantial profit.

JEFFREY'S CREEK AND OUTER HARBOR, 1887. A low tide exposes Jeffrey's Creek before its first dredging in 1896. At this time, it was more of a salt marsh than an expansive harbor, and Manchester was a quiet place.

OLIVER T. ROBERTS. Roberts and Hoare was founded by Oliver T. Roberts (1850–1922) in 1880. A descendant of one of the first settlers of Jeffrey's Creek and the son of a sea captain, he ran away from home at age 13 and worked as a cabin boy on a clipper ship. When he returned as an adult, he established his own business with William Hoare. During the building boom period of the late 1800s, the firm employed over 200 men and built hundreds of houses and town buildings. (Author's collection.)

LOBSTER COVE, 1885. Lobster Cove is typical of the many dramatic coves along the irregular Manchester coastline. This illustration shows a few of the numerous shingle-style houses built

WILLIAM HOARE. With his experience in furniture making, William Hoare (1848–1922) became a cofounder of Roberts and Hoare. Hoare contributed to the interiors, overseeing the carpenters and finish men. All the finish work was accomplished with hand tools, but these men were able to achieve a high level of craftsmanship, due in part to Manchester's long tradition of shipbuilding and cabinetmaking. (Author's collection.)

by Roberts and Hoare on Smith's Point. (Sketch by Eldon Deane, the *American Architect and Building News*, 1885.)

KRAGSYDE, BUILT IN 1882. This is a drawing of the George Nixon Black house, the famous Kragsyde. It was designed by Peabody and Stearns and continues to be the quintessential icon of the shingle style. Its organic form is reminiscent of a massive animal crouched along the rocks above the sea. It was destroyed in 1929. (Sketch by Eldon Deane, the *American Architect and Building News*, 1885.)

EXTERIOR OF KRAGSYDE, 1886. Vincent Scully, the noted architectural historian, has called Kragsyde a masterpiece. This shingle-style tour de force with neighboring houses gave Lobster Cove a magical quality. Frederick Law Olmsted designed Kragsyde's landscape. (Courtesy of *Artistic Country-Seats*, by George W. Sheldon.)

INTERIOR STAIR HALL SKETCH, KRAGSYDE, 1885. A hall with delicate interior detailing evokes the charm and sweetness of an imagined earlier Colonial era. (Sketch by Eldon Deane, the *American Architect and Building News*, 1885.)

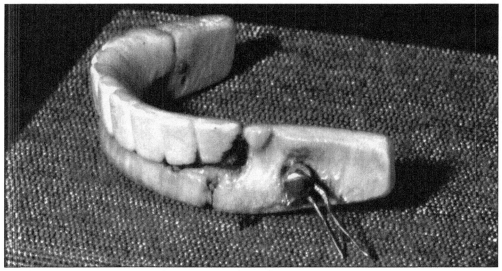

GEORGE WASHINGTON'S LATE-1700S TEETH. Black was very proud of his great-grandfather Gen. David Cobb and told many stories about his connection to Gen. George Washington during the Revolutionary War. It has been said that Black displayed a pair of Washington's false teeth in his study at Kragsyde. It is interesting to note that all of Washington's false teeth were not made of wood, as the legend states, but of ivory. (Courtesy of the National Museum of Dentistry.)

MARY HEMENWAY HOUSE, 1884. This shingle-style icon was designed by the architect William Ralph Emerson for the widow of Augustus Hemenway, Mary. Augustus had made a fortune trading with South America and China, and Mary generously used her wealth to support orphanages, Native American schools, and Boston's educational institutions. The architect sank the house into the hillside by blasting out the basement. Marianna Van Rensslaer wrote in *Century Magazine* in 1886 that the house "seems almost as much a part of nature's first intentions as do the rocks and trees themselves." (Courtesy of *Artistic Country-Seats*, by George W. Sheldon.)

FIELDS ROCK, 1882. Situated on Lobster Cove, this house was built for Richard Stone, a summer resident and prominent Boston lawyer. It is a classic shingle-style house, nestled at the head of Lobster Cove, with views of Baker's Island. (Courtesy of K. Graham.)

SKETCH OF FIELDS ROCK, 1885. The house is in close proximity to the cove. A small bridge leads to a bathing pavilion. Before the advent of swimming pools, everyone swam in the brisk ocean waters, and most homes near the sea had small wooden bathhouses in which to change. However, this one, accessible from a bridge, is certainly unique. (Sketch by Eldon Deane, the *American Architect and Building News,* 1885.

RIVER HOUSE, 1883. Designed for Rev. Cyrus Augustus Bartol, River House is one of three prominent shingled houses on Norton's Point, along with Barn House and Fort House. Over the years, River House expanded in size to accommodate additional guests and staff. In 1897,

Conover Fitch and his wife, owners of Waltham Watch Company, added a wing and doubled the size of the original house.

MANCHESTER FISHING SLOOP, C. 1884. A typical fishing sloop with an attached dory is heading out of the harbor. Notice the lack of trees in the Norton's Point landscape. A view of Fort House is on the left, and a view of River House is on the right.

BARN HOUSE, BUILT IN 1883. The design of this house was inspired by the earlier saltwater farms that were scattered about the coast of Manchester. It is located on a small, marshy inlet where in years past small fishing boats could be pulled ashore. (Sketch by Eldon Deane, the *American Architect and Building News,* 1885.)

FORT HOUSE, BUILT IN 1883. Fort House was built on the site of a War of 1812 fort, which was situated on a rocky outcrop with an unobstructed view to the mouth of the harbor. This superb house completed a village of three magnificent homes on Norton's Point and has been demolished. (Sketch by Eldon Deane, the *American Architect and Building News*, 1885.)

THE ALICE JAMES HOUSE, 1881. The Alice James house was built to look like two connected gambrel farmhouses. Its modest scale was perfect for its location on Smith's Point. It resembled an early saltwater farm, did not dominate the site, and offered a pastoral view from the yacht club across the harbor. Alice James was the sister of the author Henry James.

SANDY HOLLOW, 1880. Designed by the architect Arthur Little, this summer cottage for Rev. Cyrus Augustus Bartol was moved in 1885 to Long Beach from its original inland location on Smith's Point. The landscape near Long Beach was a low area beneath a rocky hillside and must have inspired the name Sandy Hollow.

SINGING DUNE, 1896. Located on Singing Beach, this house was built for Ethel E. Rucker of Denver, Colorado, on a strawberry patch called Tompkin's Field. It was one of the first houses built above Singing Beach. In the days before air-conditioning, all summer cottages had windows open to the sea air to take advantage of the breezes.

THE STEADMAN-HANKS HOUSE, C. 1885. Located in West Manchester, this house's first floor was built of Cape Ann granite and covered with a gambrel roof. This was a typical shingle-style combination. It is notable that Charles Steadman-Hanks, a Boston lawyer, conceived of the relatively new idea of a country club, which was originally founded as a suitable place for golf, polo, baseball, cricket, tennis, and social exchange. The clubhouse (see page 74) was built on farmland once owned by Thomas Jefferson Coolidge and is now the Essex County Club.

MANCHESTER SOCIAL OUTING, LATE 1800S. The social picnic, an English tradition, was adapted by the American upper class as a way to embrace and enjoy nature. This posed photograph tells the story of a group of people enjoying their new wealth and leisure.

AGASSIZ ROCK, LATE 1800S. A giant glacial erratic is a part of the Agassiz Rock reservation in Manchester. It is named after the celebrated naturalist Louis Agassiz. Here a solitary summer visitor, comfortably smoking his pipe, gives this giant rock interest and scale.

LABOR DAY FAMILY OUTING, 1890. The first Labor Day in Massachusetts was celebrated on the first Monday in September 1887. Informal pictures of this era were all posed, with many people making a statement about their seasonal homes and opportunities for leisure. The two men in coats and ties proudly holding oars seem to be showing their boating skills.

TUCKS POINT CHOWDER HOUSE, 1880. The picnic pavilion pictured here was built for the enjoyment of town families. Additional land was needed due to its popularity, and it was moved back several hundred yards in 1896. Notice Fort House and River House in the background. In the foreground, mothers are watching their children wade in the water, although it is unlikely that during this era the children knew how to swim.

THE MASCONOMO HOUSE, 1878. This hotel, built by Junius and Agnes Booth, was located on 12 acres of land overlooking Singing Beach. Junius was an actor and the older brother of John Wilkes Booth, infamous for assassinating Pres. Abraham Lincoln. However, this fact did not diminish the popularity of the great Masconomo House. It attracted notables, including Pres. Grover Cleveland and Lillian Russell, among others. Its massive size included 106 rooms, a dining room that seated 300 guests, and a theater. It was demolished in 1920.

MASCONOMO HOUSE PORCH, LATE 1800s. The porch that stretches across the 230-foot Masconomo House is supported by rustic cedar columns with their limbs attached. This primitive porch was symbolic of a simpler time. The woman staff member in her white dress and apron reassures the guests that they will be served with elegance and style.

TENNIS ON THE LAWN, C. 1883–1884. The Masconomo House offered several leisure activities and established the beginning of organized social sports on the North Shore. Notice the players in their "whites" and the improvised stand for the scorekeeper.

JUNIUS, EDWIN, AND JOHN WILKES BOOTH, 1864.
This photograph shows the three Booth brothers dressed for a performance of *Julius Caesar*. Junius Booth and his wife, Agnes, established the Masconomo House in 1877.

SINGING BEACH BATHHOUSES, 1884. Just beyond the lawn of the Masconomo House on Singing Beach, there is a continuous stretch of wooden bathhouses that provided families in town with a place for changing into their bathing costumes. At the time, these houses were all painted in dark green or brown in order to blend in with the landscape.

SINGING BEACH, LATE 1800S. Originally it was known as Musical Beach. The dry sand has always made a distinctive sound similar to a *zing* when walked through. This is one of only a few beaches in the world that have this particular kind of sand. Singing Beach is approximately one-half mile long, curving between two granite outcrops, one of which is the famous Eagle Head. In the 1800s, most people came for the view or to picnic, as visits to the beach in this era were quite formal.

SINGING BEACH, 1910. By this time, beachgoers are wearing white, reflective clothing, and swimming was a viable, leisurely activity. In fact, it was considered healthy by some. The beach itself was becoming more of a destination.

MANCHESTER BATH AND TENNIS CLUB, 1913. By 1913, swimming was a recognized social activity. Located on Magnolia Beach, the Manchester Bath and Tennis Club was founded for swimming and attracted bathers such as the woman in the foreground in her heavy, woolen bathing costume. By now, Manchester had three clubs: a yacht club, a golf club, and a swimming club. Most members of the Manchester summer colony belonged to all three, and if they were interested in riding and polo, they joined the Myopia Hunt Club in nearby Hamilton.

THE ESSEX COUNTY CLUB, 1893. This first clubhouse was designed by the architectural firm of Andrews, Jacques and Rantoul in the shingle style. The land, originally a farm, was owned by the Baker family prior to being purchased by Thomas Jefferson Coolidge in 1893. At the urging of Charles Steadman-Hanks, the concept of a country club offering facilities for outdoor sports for men and women became a reality. Its nine-hole golf course was managed by A. R. Campbell of St. Andrews, Scotland.

BEATRIX HOYT, DRIVING FROM SEVENTH TEE, 1897. Beatrix Hoyt, with her good form, won all her matches at the women's national amateur finals. She had margins of six strokes over her nearest competitor and claimed the women's open championship at the Essex County Club.

MARGARET CURTIS, 1896. At age 12, Margaret Curtis (third from left) competed in the 1896 Essex County Club Women's Club Championship. Margaret and her sister Harriet went on to become legends in women's golf and tennis. With the advent of country clubs, women were able to compete and be active participants in many sports.

SHEEP AT ESSEX COUNTY CLUB, 1898. The grass on the nine-hole course of the original clubhouse was cropped for the first six years by a flock of three dozen sheep.

HIGHWOOD TERRACE FACADE, 1897. Highwood, owned by William B. Walker, was Manchester's largest summer estate. Walker was a millionaire who made his fortune in Chicago real estate and the stock market. As the social life of Manchester became more established, the early impulse to escape to the simple life changed and with this also came changes in architectural styles. This estate is reminiscent of the massive English country homes that were situated in stunning natural settings.

HIGHWOOD ENTRANCE FACADE, 1897. This English Tudor–style house was sited on top of one of Manchester's highest hills and required its own water tower. The landscape was designed by the Olmsted Brothers firm of Brookline, and the forested grounds were covered by over seven miles of roadways and horse trails. Additional structures on the property were stables, outbuildings, a car garage, greenhouses, caretakers' homes, and gardeners' cottages.

FRONT ENTRANCE OF HIGHWOOD, 1897. Mrs. Walker and her father, Mr. Cobb, pose in the front entry. Notice the quality of the workmanship, evident in the area where Walker and her father are seated.

SOCIAL GUESTS, C. 1900. Mr. and Mrs. William B. Walker (on the left) are welcoming unidentified summer guests on the terrace of Highwood.

WOODHOLM, NEO-GEORGIAN CONSERVATORY AND GREENHOUSES, C. 1900. Woodholm was the property of William B. Walker's son Charles Cobb Walker. The Woodholm property adjoined Highwood and became one massive estate when Charles inherited Highwood from his father.

INTERIOR ELEVATION, WOODHOLM GREENHOUSE, C. 1900. Families of the Gilded Age prided themselves in their gardens and their gardeners, who maintained the natural beauty of the estates and raised prizewinning flowers. Most of these gardeners were given their own private cottages.

WALKER ESTATE, 1897. The property included miles of woodland walking and riding trails throughout. Notice the lights that illuminate the path. Trails like this one were meticulously maintained by crews directed by the estate manager.

HORSE AND CARRIAGE TRAILS, C. 1922. Helen Kitfield Roberts enjoys an outing on the Walker estate riding trails, which were maintained by Canadian forestry crews. Notice the manicured lawn on the sides of the path. (Author's collection.)

ROBERTS AND HOARE MILL, 1885. Roberts and Hoare occupied a large section of downtown Manchester. This view shows a portion of the business's establishment. Roberts and Hoare became one of the most respected and successful building contractors in the country. By 1895, the partners had built 32 houses and 21 stables for summer residents, and by the dawn of the 20th century, 10 projects were often underway at once.

VIEW OF SMITH'S POINT FROM NORTON'S POINT, C. 1890. Looking across the harbor to Smith's Point, the effects of extensive building on what was once the open land of Smith's farm is visible.

KNIGHT'S WHARF ON THE INNER HARBOR, 1885. Lumber, delivered by train and off-loaded onto barges, was piled at this wharf. At the busiest times, train loads of lumber were backed up as far as Beverly. Downtown Manchester and the inner harbor was a staging area for all the construction materials needed to satisfy the huge demand for new buildings.

Notice the rocky granite outcrops, which must have been a challenge to new construction. Today trees hide many of these properties.

SUNNYBANK BUILDING SITE, 1899. A steam-powered drill, shown on the left, has been hauled to the site in preparation for blasting a cellar. All the foundation work, prior to World War II, was built from rubble stone, quarried, or blasted from the building site.

SUNNYBANK FROM THE HARBOR, 1901. This large 26-room summer cottage on Gales Point was designed by architects Everett and Meade in 1896 for Albert I. Croll of Boston. It was one of the last of the great shingled houses and a transitional building between the organic shingle style and the newly popular Tudor style.

THE ROCKS, 1903. The Rocks was built in the grand Tudor style for Eben Dyer Jordan Jr., whose father established Jordan Marsh and Company in the mid-19th century. Eben Jr., a contributor to the Boston cultural community, built Jordan Hall and the Boston Opera House and was president of the New England Conservatory of Music.

THE ROCKS, MUSIC ROOM EXTERIOR, 1903. Here a dramatic brick chimney rises out of the back side of the music room, making a strong visual statement when viewed from the water. Powerful architectural elements such as this one have contributed to Manchester's unique identity.

UNDERCLIFF, 1900. Undercliff was named for its formal gardens carved out of the side of a granite cliff by the sea. This stucco Tudor-style house was built for Charles Head. The elevation shows the curved sunroom facing the ocean.

UNDERCLIFF OCEAN FACADE, 1900. Undercliff and its terrace are situated on the rocky coastline of Graves Beach and face Graves Island. This island was available to visitors walking to it at low tide for picnics, but they had to watch the tides carefully or they would be easily stranded. This Tudor estate shows the influence of a well-traveled leisure class that was particularly influenced by the building styles of England and parts of Europe.

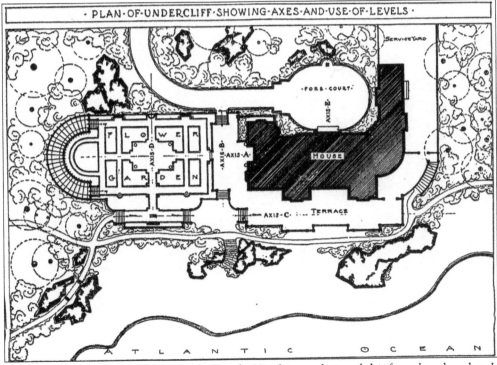

UNDERCLIFF SITE PLAN, 1900. Martha Brooks Hutchinson designed this formal garden plan. It is interesting that the symmetry of this classical garden was juxtaposed to a Tudor building.

HENRY WADSWORTH LONGFELLOW, 1868. A longtime visitor to Manchester-by-the-Sea, Henry Wadsworth Longfellow was one of many famous literary notables to frequent the Thunderbolt Hill home of James and Annie Fields. James Fields founded the *Atlantic Monthly* and published the works of his Manchester summer guests, including Longfellow, Nathaniel Hawthorne, Ralph Waldo Emerson, John Greenleaf Whittier, Harriet Beecher Stowe, and Lucy Larcom. (Courtesy of the Maine Historical Society.)

FELSENMERE, 1901. This estate was built on land originally owned by Richard Henry Dana Sr., Manchester's first summer resident and founder of the *North American Review*. His son William Henry Dana Sr. wrote the book *Two Years before the Mast*, published in 1840. Richard Henry Dana III sold a portion of their land to the Caner family in 1899. It was common to give these large cottages a name. Felsenmere is German for "field and sea."

CROWHURST, 1905. Crowhurst was designed by owner Francis Meredith Whitehouse, who developed the property in stages. The first stage was a farm, and then a decade later, the main house, Crowhurst, was built in the Norman French style. The scale of this house was huge. The dining room alone was the size of a typical Cape Cod cottage, measuring 20 feet wide by 30 feet long.

COVE FARM, 1895. Cove Farm was designed by Whitehouse and built to complement his Norman French–style estate, Crowhurst. The charming assembly of towers, stables, and a courtyard were built in the same style as the main house. Whitehouse and his wife lived on this model working farm during the construction of the main house. This arrangement of buildings along the ocean and marsh created a view of a medieval village from Crowhurst.

LOGGIA OF THE THOMAS JEFFERSON COOLIDGE HOUSE, 1904. This marble palace was designed by McKim, Meade and White in the spirit of the Newport mansions for Thomas Jefferson Coolidge, a great-great-grandson of Thomas Jefferson. Coolidge was a generous benefactor to Manchester, funding many of its public buildings, including the Memorial Hall Library. He was also one of the founders of the Essex County Club.

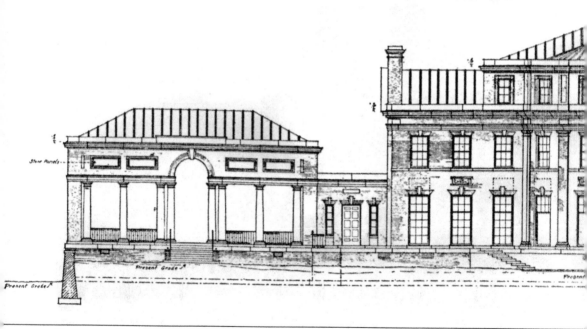

OCEANSIDE FACADE OF THE THOMAS JEFFERSON COOLIDGE HOUSE, 1904. McKim, Meade and White designed this mansion in the fashionable classical style. Their recent work at the 1893 World's Columbian Exposition in Chicago had an enormous influence in their design of new homes for the wealthy. The exposition established the classical vocabulary for public architecture and

ENTRANCE FACADE OF THE THOMAS JEFFERSON COOLIDGE HOUSE, 1904. The elegant brick mansion with its marble columns was a precursor to the popular Colonial Revival style that was prevalent in Manchester at the dawn of the 20th century. Manchester residents were no longer simple rusticators escaping the city. This Gilded Age entrance reflects the importance placed on social position and society during this era.

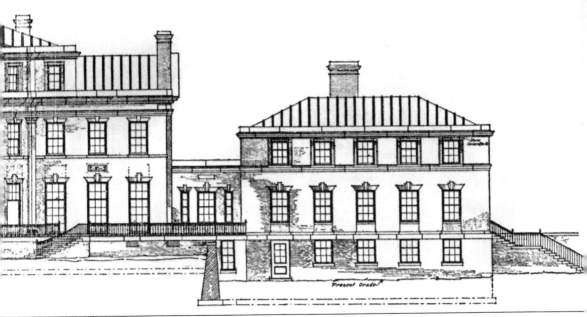

the great summerhouses of Newport, Rhode Island, as well as this one in Manchester-by-the-Sea. (Courtesy of *Monograph of the Work of McKim, Meade and White, 1879–1915.*)

ALL OAKES, 1903. This summer residence was built for Edward S. Grew. Similar in style to the brick Thomas Jefferson Coolidge house, this grand house differed in that it was built entirely of wood. All Oakes was situated on a high point at the entrance to Manchester's harbor. Massive houses like these in the classical style were a major departure from the earlier eclectic and casual arts and crafts style of the shingled cottages. The Olmsted Brothers designed the landscape.

ALL OAKES INTERIOR, 1903. This elaborate Colonial Revival interior indicates a fascination with a fictitious version of history. It was a stage set or fantasy of Colonial America on a grand scale. The emerging Colonial Revival style created a unifying identity for established New England families. This new idealized version of the Colonial past came with butlers, maids, cooks, gardeners, and grooms.

FASHIONABLE WOMAN, C. 1900. This elaborately beaded gown is typical of that worn by wealthy society women in the Gilded Age. This dress may have come from Paris, as attire was extremely formal for the lavish events attended by the socially prominent. Great care was taken with the details of entertaining, which included dress, table settings, flowers, and the complex pairings of food with wine. Entertaining on a grand scale in Manchester by-the-Sea's opulent mansions continued into the early 1920s. (Author's collection.)

CLIPSTON, 1898. Built for Mortimer B. Mason on Smith's Point with a sweeping view of the harbor, this Colonial Revival mansion was designed with a massive drawing room for entertaining on a large scale. A vast porch running across the entire back of the house provided an ideal space for summer entertaining. Formal gardens were accessed from the porch.

MINK COTTAGE, 1899. This house, almost near completion, was designed for Oliver W. Mink. A group of painters have just finished painting the house white. The Mink Cottage was large for its relatively small lot. Landscape architect Fletcher Steele designed a magnificent walled garden that created an expanded sense of space.

APPLE TREES, 1895. Apple Trees was built for Gerard Bement and subsequently purchased by Stephen Crosby in 1903. The Crosbys added a sunken garden, greenhouses, and additions to their carriage house. The interior is a magnificent example of Colonial Revival at its best.

FABYAN-GREW-ODMAN HOUSE, C. 1900. Built in West Manchester in the Colonial Revival style, this house's genius is in its simplicity of plan and its location in a Frederick Law Olmsted landscape. From the street, one sees only a classical portico that covers a rectangular building designed to become a backdrop for its landscape. (Courtesy of *Summer Echoes from the 19th Century, Manchester-by-the-Sea*, by Elsie P. Youngman and photographer George M. Cushing.)

EAGLIS, 1892. Eaglis on Gale's Point was built on what was an open hay field for the Smith farm, known as Gale's Point Field. It was built for N. Helen Paramore of St. Louis. This point of land is a dramatic natural breakwater for Manchester's protected harbor. The house, originally built in the shingle style, now boasts Colonial Revival interiors.

THE CLIFFS, 1880. This house was built for George Dudley Howe. It shows the influence of the Centennial Exposition in Philadelphia in 1876, where a new interest in American Colonial architecture was revived. Its scale and location on a rocky outcrop by the sea, as well as a substantial porch, gives it a comfortable, appealing quality. (Courtesy of *Artistic Country-Seats,* by George W. Sheldon.)

THE CLIFFS INTERIOR, 1880. The detail of this front entry hall is restrained when compared to similar homes of this period. The emphasis is on a casual comfort while at the same time having the symbols of understated social prestige. (Author's collection.)

THE CLIFFS CARRIAGE HOUSE, 1880. This Colonial Revival carriage house has an interesting dormered porch on the roof for loading hay into the loft. It provided space for four to six horses and numerous carriages of different sizes. (Author's collection.)

YOUNG MAN IN GIG, C. 1910. In its day, a carriage called a gig was the equivalent of today's young man's sports car. (Author's collection.)

ELSINAES, 1899. Elsinaes was redesigned and built for Elsie Forbes Perkins Hooper, one of the first of the seasonal summer people to become a full-time resident. She loved to build and added many additions to her home with architectural styles ranging from medieval to Colonial Revival. Notice the Colonial Revival tower on the top of the building. It was accessed by one of the many secret doors installed in the house.

THE ISLAND WITH THE CHARLES READ HOUSE, 1890. Before the harbor was dredged, this site, called the island, was the town landing where shallow draft boats could off-load supplies to be stored in a post and beam barn. Originally built around 1800, this barn was renovated for Charles Read in the Colonial Revival style. As Manchester became a more popular summer destination, additions were made to accommodate frequent guests and a larger staff.

LITTLE ORCHARD, RENOVATED, C. 1900. Originally an early Kitfield house, Little Orchard was remodeled in the Colonial Revival style for Roland C. Lincoln by architect Joseph Chandler. This unique property has been accepted into the stewardship program of Historic New England. The present owner is a direct descendant of Sir Richard Saltonstall, one of the original grantees of the Massachusetts Bay Company and who arrived on the *Arbella* in 1630.

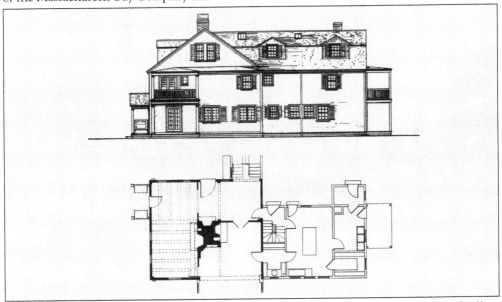

PEARSE-MAY HOUSE, ELEVATION AND PLAN, RENOVATED, 1905. This early-Colonial dwelling was to become a summer home for George Allen, a Salem sea captain and financier. Chandler was chosen to be the architect for his reputation in Colonial Revival renovation and his work on the Paul Revere house, the old statehouse, and the House of Seven Gables. Here the familiar Pearse-May house (see page 20) was completely remodeled in the Colonial Revival style. (Author's collection.)

VIEW OF THE HARBOR AND THE MOORINGS, NORTON'S POINT, 1900. By 1900, the amount of building on Smith's Point had dramatically increased, along with the size of the harbor, which had been dredged to provide deepwater moorings for large pleasure yachts. The harbor looks much the same today.

THE MOORINGS, C. 1900. This summer cottage was originally built as Barn House in 1883 (see page 64). It was altered within a short time after its construction, and numerous additions were built to accommodate an increasing number of guests. From sketches and pictures taken by successive owners, it appears that additions occurred on a regular basis through the 1920s, steadily evolving into a large Colonial Revival–style mansion.

VIEW FROM THE MOORINGS LAWN, 1910. The rotunda and the Manchester Yacht Club are viewed from the house and lawn. As the house grew in size, the landscape expanded to include extensive formal gardens.

THE MOORINGS BOATHOUSE, 1905. This is a classic summer scene, with the large rambling shingled house in the background and a boathouse that looks like a tiny yacht club. Servants stand by the door to assist the guests returning from a day's sail.

LADIES IN A GARDEN, C. 1900. The women are identified as a Mrs. Foote and Diana Ward Rockwell. All of these estates had massive formal gardens. Much of the natural landscape that drew the first summer residents was swept aside to build elaborate formal gardens that required gardeners and extensive greenhouses. The earlier landscaping used indigenous plant material that was adaptable to the salty, rocky coastline. Gardeners competed for trophies in elaborate flower shows. A horticultural hall was built in Manchester to accommodate these well-attended events.

THE MOORINGS FORMAL GARDEN, C. 1910. This view shows the Italian gardens with Whitter's Creek and Tucks Point in the distance. They were built on filled-in marshland that covered several acres. These gardens were a showplace of the North Shore and visited by Pres. Woodrow Wilson and his wife Edith in 1917.

VIEW OF THE GARDENS AT UNDERCLIFF, 1902. As the landscape architect for Undercliff (see pages 84 and 85), Martha Brooks Hutchinson was one of the leading females in her profession at the time. She believed that it was possible to create a logical system of relationships among house, garden, and surrounding landscape to create inviting and mysterious vistas and views.

THE CHIMNEY'S GARDEN, 1906. These formal Italian gardens were designed by Frederick Law Olmsted Jr., the son of the famous Frederick Law Olmsted, who designed Central Park in New York. In the formal garden plan, there were numerous pools for aquatic plants and fish.

MANCHESTER YACHT CLUB, 1892. As yachting was now a popular pastime, massive clubhouses were built throughout the North Shore. Meals and alcohol were served, and they became social as well as sailing clubs. Running contrary to this trend, the founders of the Manchester Yacht Club built a modest structure in 1892 to keep the focus on sailing as its primary purpose.

TUCKS POINT ROTUNDA, 1896. The unique rotunda was designed for the people of the town of Manchester. With the construction of the new yacht club at Tucks Point, the view from the town's chowder house was now blocked. In response, the town built a new structure to recapture the lost harbor view. The completed rotunda, built in the classical style, complements the yacht club and has become Manchester's iconic landmark.

Yacht Race off Baker's Island Light,
Manchester-by-the-Sea.

YACHT RACE OFF BAKER'S ISLAND, C. 1900. As early as 1904, 81 yachts were listed as owned by members of the Manchester Yacht Club. It was this interest in yachting that had encouraged E. P. Crocker to open a boatyard in 1892 and David Fenton and Timothy White to open a second one in 1895. The racing yachts in this picture were built locally, and their designs were based on the swift fishing schooners. Races were held regularly off the coast of Manchester.

RACING SCOW, 1910. The Crocker and Fenton and White boatyards built numerous successful racing boats, one of which was called a scow. They were flat bottomed, 40 to 50 feet long overall, without ballast, and carried 130-pound bronze bilge boards for stability. In this picture, four yachtsmen are sailing a scow in Manchester waters. (Courtesy of the Essex Shipbuilding Museum, Dana Story Collection.)

SCHOONER, C. 1900. This schooner, typical of those raced by the summer residents around 1900, was also a popular cruising boat. For Manchester yachtsmen, Maine was often a favorite destination. (Courtesy of the Essex Shipbuilding Museum, Dana Story Collection.)

SPEEDBOAT *PETER PAN*, C. 1915. With the advent of a practical, marine internal combustion engine, sails were no longer an absolute necessity. Marblehead was now a short boat ride away. (Author's collection.)

THE CORSAIR, 1899.
Financier J. P. Morgan arrived
with staff and family aboard
the *Corsair* for many summer
seasons. This steam-powered
yacht, with a length of
304 feet and a draft of 18 feet,
had to be moored offshore at
the entrance to the harbor.

STEAM YACHT CORSAIR
Length 304 feet
Designed by J. Beavor Webb and *built by* T. S. Marvel in 1899
for J. Pierpont Morgan

THE AZTEC, 1902. Another steam-powered yacht, the *Aztec* measured 206 feet and was owned
by longtime summer resident Albert C. Burrage. For 40 years, the yacht was often moored in
Manchester's outer harbor. The *Aztec* served in both world wars.

ESSEX COUNTY CLUB, 1909. As the summer population grew, the Essex County Club made numerous additions to the original shingle-style clubhouse. By 1909, the club's orientation had changed to have a 22-foot-deep, 240-foot-long porch, with a view of the croquet circle and tennis courts. The clubhouse was now sporting the Colonial Revival colors of yellow with white trim.

PRES. WOODROW WILSON, C. 1915. Pres. Woodrow Wilson spent summers in Manchester during World War I and enjoyed playing golf at the Essex County Club. He was an avid golfer and is famously quoted as saying, "Golf is a game in which one endeavors to control a ball with implements ill adapted for the purpose." He is also known to have used black golf balls when playing on snow. (Courtesy of the Woodrow Wilson Presidential Library.)

Proposed New Clubhouse, 1913. A fire completely destroyed the Essex County Club clubhouse in 1913. This is a rendering of the new Georgian-style building. It was completed in 1915, and except for minor changes, the clubhouse remains the same today. (Author's collection.)

Pres. William Howard Taft, 1925. Pres. William Howard Taft, an honorary member of the Essex County Club, was one of many celebrities who enjoyed golfing during the summer season. Other notables included J. P. Morgan, King Leopold of Belgium, Al Jolson, and Bing Crosby. (Courtesy of the Library of Congress.)

WRIGHT FLYER OVER SINGING BEACH, C. 1905. By the early 1900s, new machines were becoming a part of daily life. However, these people seem unimpressed by the new invention flying above

them. The photographer's double exposure of two separate events explains their disinterest.

THE CIRCLE AT SINGING BEACH, C. 1908. Horses were beginning to share the roadways with automobiles. Notice the family bathhouses, which remained on the beach until the hurricane of 1933, when all were swept into the sea.

CARS GATHERED AT BEACH STREET, 1910. As this photograph suggests, the automobile is increasing in popularity due to its availability, although it is clearly still a novelty. Notice that all the drivers are seated on the right.

Six

The Village

CENTRAL STREET, 1890. By 1890, Manchester had become a substantial town. In the distance are, from left to right, Sheldon's Market, the fire station, the Manchester House (second from right), and the Rabardy Block, which housed a variety store, the post office, and the telegraph office. By this time, the Bingham house (near right), had been converted to commercial use, and the town was burgeoning to support the ever-growing summer colony.

VIEW OF THE HARBOR, 1915. Compared with an earlier view in 1887 (see page 55), the harbor is now completely dredged. The sandstone Richardsonian-style railroad station was built in 1896. Standley's Blacksmith Shop is on the right. Smith's Point (far left) is no longer a pasture and is populated by summer cottages.

FLOYD'S NEWSSTAND, 1903. Julius Rabardy, who started a variety store in 1865, went into business with Lyman Floyd, a candy confectioner. In 1884, Floyd moved with Rabardy to a new building, which still stands today and is known as the Rabardy Block. Floyd's candy shop and newsstand was the birthplace of a favorite Manchester tradition. Alice Rice, a descendant of both Floyd and Rabardy, sold Floyd's penny candy to the children of Manchester until her death in 2007.

MANCHESTER FIRE STATION, 1892. The fire department was housed in a unique Victorian structure on School Street. It had a balcony for Saturday night band concerts and a big brass whistle on the roof that was powered by a steam generator in the basement. The previous fire station located on the common was readapted for use as the police station.

1. EDWARD P. FLYNN.
2. HOWARD M. STANLEY.
3. ARTHUR A. SMOTHERS.
4. JOHN E. RIGGS.
5. SUMNER A. MASON.
6. MICHAEL J. KELLEHER.
7. JAMES P. READ.
8. JAMES A. KEHOE.
9. HERMAN C. SWETT.
10. CHARLES C. DODGE.
11. LOUIS O. LATIONS.
12. ALFRED E. HERSEY.
13. ELLERY L. ROGERS (CAPT).
14. CHARLES E. CHADWICK.
15. THOMAS A. BAKER (ASST. CHIEF)
16. FRANK L. FLOYD.
17. WILLIAM H. ALLEN.
18. CHESTER D. COOK.
19. MANUEL S. MIGUEL.
20. RALPH H. LANE.
21. BENJAMIN L. STANLE[

MANCHESTER FIREFIGHTERS, 1914. On June 25, 1914, Manchester responded to the great Salem fire. This photograph shows the heroes shortly after the event in front of the firehouse and steam pumper Seaside No. 2, which is now located in the restored 1885 Seaside No. 1 Station Museum, located on the common.

PUMPING STATION AND WELL AT THE WATER DEPARTMENT, 1892. These interesting, lyrical buildings are a celebration of the distribution of water throughout the town. The conical-shaped roof to the left is the well cover over the water source. The building to the right contains a steam-powered pump that delivers water to the standpipe on the hill in the background. From there, it flows by gravity to the homes in town. When the system was completed, there was a water celebration that included a parade, a boat procession in the harbor, and a band concert.

AGNES BOOTH SCHOEFFEL, 1892. Married for a third time, Agnes Booth Schoeffel, owner of the Masconomo House (see page 70), sits in a Victorian carriage decorated in pink and white asters with matching ribbons. She is about to be in a parade celebrating the opening of the town's water supply. She was awarded first prize.

ELECTRIC COMPANY, 1903. Until the dawn of the 20th century, the town was lit by gas lamps, and kerosene was used for home lighting. In 1903, the town built the Manchester Electric Company. Most of the wiring went underground to preserve the beauty of the town, and by 1915, the town streets were illuminated by electricity. Perhaps this very stolid classical building reflects the town's desire to keep people safe from this new invention. (Author's collection.)

HORTICULTURAL HALL, 1917. In the era of the great summer cottages, this building was the site of the annual flower show where estate gardeners competed for prizes. The hall was a home for many town civic organizations. It had a stage for theatrical productions, served as a movie theater, and provided a meeting place for young and old. The building was demolished in 1963.

BACHRACH STUDIO, 1925. This whimsical English cottage is located at the corner of Bridge and Bennett Streets and housed a branch of the famous Bachrach photography studio. At the height of the summer season, the studio was in great demand for formal portraiture and to record the numerous important social events. (Author's collection.)

BOY SCOUTS OF AMERICA TROOP 3 HOUSE, 1915. The Boy Scouts was founded in the United States in 1910. Manchester's Troop 3, organized in 1915, was one of the first in the area. This was the era of the Scout movement, started in England by Robert Baden-Powell. Here Troop 3 is assembled in front of its rather elegant Greek Revival house. By the 1920s, the troop built another house on School Street.

Seven

THE END OF AN ERA

FOURTH OF JULY PARADE, 1915. Representing enlisted troops from all the wars beginning with the Revolutionary War to the start of World War I, these men pose before marching in the annual Fourth of July parade. (Author's collection.)

WORLD WAR I VICTORY GARDEN, C. 1918. One of the immediate effects on Manchester following America's entry into World War I in 1917 was the unavailability of food. Many residents had a victory garden and probably some chickens. Residents without adequate land for a garden used a common field. When the war concluded, fortunes were made by the wealthy during the Roaring Twenties when fun and lightness prevailed. By 1929, it all came to an end. With the debilitating hardships of the Depression, Manchester's summer colony went into decline.

EARLY OBSERVATION TOWER, 1942. Located in the village on top of the town hill, the observation tower was a part of the nation's first line of defense against enemy aircraft. As there was no radar, it was manned 24 hours a day. The small tower to the right was hastily built in 1940 prior to the United States' entry into the war.

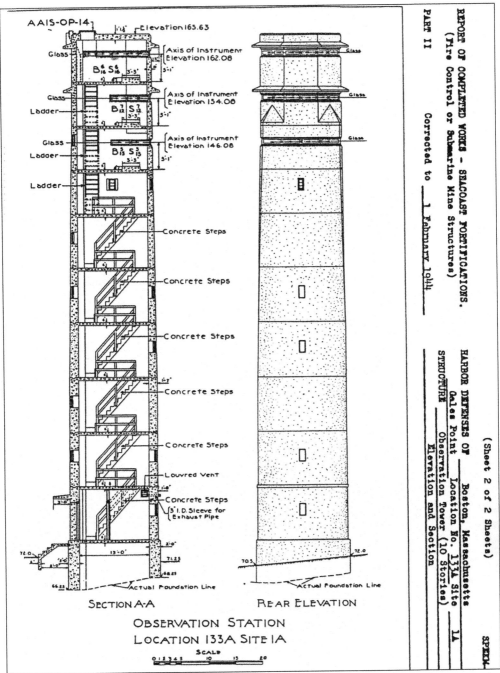

REPORT OF COMPLETED WORKS — SEACOAST FORTIFICATIONS.
(Fire Control or Submarine Mine Structures)

PART II   Corrected to   1 February 1944

(Sheet 2 of 2 Sheets)

HARBOR DEFENSES OF   Boston, Massachusetts
Gales Point   Location No. 133A Site
STRUCTURE   Observation Tower (10 Stories)
Elevation and Section   1A

SPECIAL

AAIS-OP-14
Elevation 165.63

Glass
Axis of Instrument
Elevation 162.08
B¹⁶S¹⁶   3'-3'   5'-1'

Glass
Ladder
B¹⁵S¹⁵   Axis of Instrument
Elevation 154.08
5'-1'

Glass
Ladder
B¹⁴S¹⁴   Axis of Instrument
Elevation 146.08
3'-3'   5'-1'

Ladder

Concrete Steps

Concrete Steps

Concrete Steps

Concrete Steps

Concrete Steps

Louvred Vent

Concrete Steps

3' I.D. Sleeve for
Exhaust Pipe

13'-0'   2'-0'
72.0   71.83   2'-0'
1'-0'
66.25   68.83
Actual Foundation Line

SECTION A-A

Glass

Glass

Glass

70.5   72.0
Actual Foundation Line

REAR ELEVATION

OBSERVATION STATION
LOCATION 133A SITE 1A

SCALE
0 1 2 3 4 5   10   15   20

OBSERVATION TOWER ELEVATION AND SECTION, 1944. As America was being drawn into the emerging World War II conflict, high surveillance towers were being erected in Manchester. This concrete tower is located near the Howe estate (see page 94) on Smith's Point. The tower and others like it were part of the Boston Harbor Defense Command, enabling coastal artillery to accurately locate distant targets. German U-boats cruised in Massachusetts Bay waters and occasionally parts of their remains washed up on Manchester's beaches. (Courtesy of Craig Lentz.)

U.S. NAVY SUBCHASER, 1943. By 1942, Nazi submarines were sinking tankers and merchant vessels off the coast faster than they could be replaced. The navy contracted with the Calderwood Shipyard to build eight wooden subchasers to be part of a 438-boat fleet. The building of yachts had shifted to intensive building of warships for the navy.

FOURTH OF JULY BONFIRE. At the conclusion of World War II, Manchester, along with the rest of the country, had a lot to celebrate. This picture, taken in 1976, is similar to the mammoth pyre that was constructed on the edge of the harbor at Masconomo Park in 1946. At the time the bonfire was part of one of the longest Fourth of July programs in the history of the town. This Independence Day celebration was honoring America's contribution to the Allied victory. (Author's collection.)

THE OLD CORNER INN, 1930s. Built around an earlier 18th-century home, this enlarged house served as a foreign embassy during the Gilded Age in Manchester. After World War II, it reopened as the Old Corner Inn. As times changed, people were more mobile, and a short vacation was popular in this charming guesthouse. By the 1930s, the massive Masconomo House was no longer a destination and was demolished, as were many of the grand summer hotels in New England. (Author's collection.)

OBSERVATION TOWER RENOVATION, C. 1994. The 10-story gray concrete observation tower and the barracks building at its base was a vestige of World War II. It was declared government surplus and sold for $29,400 in the early 1950s. An enterprising owner built a fine new home at its base, and the tower became a lighthouse. It is now an attractive coastal landmark. (Author's collection.)

DEMOLITION OF THE 1892 FIRE STATION, 1974. After World War II, many unique old buildings were demolished, one of which was the Manchester Fire Station. (Author's collection.)

DEMOLITION OF TOWN HALL, 1969. With the demolition of the town hall, it seemed as if the destruction of historic town buildings was becoming a fad. By 1963, both the horticultural hall and the railroad station had been torn down. (Courtesy of Dick Towle.)

Eight

RENEWAL

SEASIDE NO. 1, 1885. In light of the architectural losses that have been incurred throughout Manchester, there seems to be a developing appreciation of the town's unique history. A good example is the community's involvement and commitment to the restoration of Seaside No. 1 when it was threatened with demolition. This Colonial Revival structure was built as a firehouse and then served as a police station for 75 years. (Courtesy of Historic New England.)

HEMENWAY HOUSE BEFORE RENOVATION, C. 1974. The Hemenway house was typical of many great summer estates that could only function with a full-time staff (see page 60). The Manchester area had never fully recovered from the Depression, and the old summer families were selling off their houses, tearing them down, or modifying them beyond recognition. When this property was purchased, it was in serious disrepair. (Author's collection.)

HEMENWAY HOUSE AFTER RENOVATION, 1992. As the building had been seriously neglected, it required extensive rebuilding of the features that made this William Ralph Emerson house an architectural icon of the shingle style. It required new infrastructure, modern conveniences, and extensive renovations, completed by Stephen Roberts Holt. (Author's collection.)

FIELDS ROCK RECONSTRUCTION, BEFORE 1951. During the 1950s and 1960s, if a large summer cottage was not torn down, it was modified beyond recognition by lopping off the top floors, dormers, and towers. It was, in part, simply a modernist reflex that all but destroyed many of the great houses in Manchester. Fields Rock (see page 61) was once a grand shingle-style cottage on Lobster Cove that was situated near the demolished Kragsyde (see page 58). (Author's collection.)

FIELDS ROCK REBUILT, 2007. This reinvented house, designed by the author, although not an exact replica, is built in the spirit of the original structure. Arthur Little's plan was well suited to the site, with a magnificent view of Lobster Cove. (Author's collection.)

THE MOORINGS BEFORE RECONSTRUCTION, 1999. Originally called Barn House (see page 64), this house was later enlarged in the Colonial Revival style to become the Moorings (see page 98). A 1979 renovation in the modernist style stripped the Moorings of all its elaborate character. It was completely torn down, with the exception of the original central block. (Author's collection.)

THE MOORINGS REBUILT, 2001. This reinvention of the Moorings, designed by the author, was made possible by the current owners' interest in the historic significance of what was left of the original structure. They could have demolished what remained, as so many others have done, but instead, they made a substantial contribution to the integrity of the harbor and the town of Manchester-by-the-Sea. (Author's collection.)

SUNNYBANK RENOVATION, 1994. This historic home (see page 82) miraculously survived the destruction of the 1950s and 1960s. It was redesigned by the author for a family that appreciated the historic character of this house and its importance to Manchester's coastline. Without affecting its architectural integrity, changes were made to accommodate a contemporary lifestyle. (Author's collection.)

NEW HOUSE, 2001. The original shingle-style Steadman-Hanks house (see page 67) had been demolished, but the remains of a horse barn and carriage house inspired the design for the new project. The owners wanted an authentic shingle-style house, and this was accomplished with the incorporation of the original barn frame. Their efforts have created a Gilded Age summer cottage named Seacroft on the original site. It was designed by the author. (Author's collection.)

Visit us at
arcadiapublishing.com

CPSIA information can be obtained
at www.ICGtesting.com
Printed in the USA
LVOW05*0717110117
520557LV00016B/64/P